SIR THOMAS BROWNE

The greatest of these is charity.

SIR THOMAS BROWNE

an *Appreciation*

with some of the best passages of the Physician's Writings selected and arranged by

Alexander Whyte

Religio Medici
Printed for Andrew Crooke : 1642

KENNIKAT PRESS
Port Washington, N. Y./London

SIR THOMAS BROWN

First published in 1898
Reissued in 1971 by Kennikat Press
Library of Congress Catalog Card No: 71-118556
ISBN 0-8046-1181-5

Manufactured by Taylor Publishing Company   Dallas, Texas

DEDICATED TO

SIR THOMAS GRAINGER STEWART

PRESIDENT OF THE BRITISH MEDICAL ASSOCIATION

AT WHOSE REQUEST THIS APPRECIATION WAS DELIVERED AS

THE INAUGURAL DISCOURSE

AT THE OPENING MEETING OF THE ASSOCIATION

IN ST. GILES' CATHEDRAL ON THE 26TH JULY 1898

IN GREAT GOOD-WILL AND LOVE BY

ALEXANDER WHYTE

CONTENTS

APPRECIATION AND INTRODUCTION

APPRECIATION
AND INTRODUCTION

THE *Religio Medici* is a universally recognised
English classic. And the *Urn-Burial*, the
Christian Morals, and the *Letter to a Friend*
are all quite worthy to take their stand beside
the *Religio Medici*. Sir Thomas Browne made
several other contributions to English literature besides these masterpieces; but it is on
the *Religio Medici*, and on what Sir Thomas
himself calls 'other pieces of affinity thereto,'
that his sure fame as a writer of noble truth
and stately English most securely rests. Sir
Thomas Browne was a physician of high stand-
ing and large practice all his days; and he was
an antiquarian and scientific writer of the
foremost information and authority : but it is
the extraordinary depth and riches and imagina-
tive sweep of his mind, and his rare wisdom
and wealth of heart, and his quite wonderful
English style, that have all combined together

to seal Sir Thomas Browne with his well-earned
immortality.

Sir Thomas Browne's outward life can be
told in a very few words. He was born at
London in 1605. He lost his father very
early, and it must have been a very great loss.
For the old mercer was wont to creep up to
his little son's cradle when he was asleep, and
uncover and kiss the child's breast, and pray,
' as 'tis said of Origen's father, that the Holy
Ghost would at once take possession there.'
The old merchant was able to leave money
enough to take his gifted son first to Win-
chester School, and then to Oxford, where he
graduated in New Pembroke in 1626. On
young Browne's graduation, old Anthony à
Wood has this remark, that those who love
Pembroke best can wish it nothing better than
that it may long proceed as it has thus begun.
As soon as he had taken his university degree
young Browne entered on the study of
medicine : and, in pursuit of that fast-rising
science, he visited and studied in the most
famous schools of France and Italy and Holland.
After various changes of residence, through all
of which it is somewhat difficult to trace the
young physician's movements, we find him at
last fairly settled in the city of Norwich, where

he spent the remainder of his long, and busy, and prosperous, and honourable life.

Dr. Johnson laments that Sir Thomas Browne has left us no record of his travels and studies abroad, and all Sir Thomas's readers will join with his great biographer in that regret. At the same time, as we turn over the pile of letters that Sir Thomas sent to his student son Edward, and to his sailor son Thomas, when they were abroad at school and on ship, we can easily collect and picture to ourselves the life that the writer of those so wise and so beautiful letters led when he himself was still a student at Montpellier and Padua and Leyden. 'Honest Tom,—God bless thee, and protect thee, and mercifully lead thee through the ways of His providence. Be diligent in going to church. Be constant, and not negligent in your daily private prayers. Be a good husband. Cast up your accounts with all care. Be temperate in diet, and be wary not to over-heat yourself. Be courteous and civil to all. Live with an apothecary, and observe his drugs and practice. Frequent civil company. Point your letters, and put periods at the ends of your sentences. Have the love and the fear of God ever before your eyes. And may God confirm your faith in Christ. Observe the

manner of trade : how they make wine and
vinegar, and keep a note of all that for me.
Be courteous and humble in all your conversation, and of good manners : which he that
learneth not in France travaileth in vain.
When at sea read good books. Without good
books time cannot be well spent in those great
ships. Learn the stars also : the particular
coasts : the depth of the road-steads : and the
risings and fallings of the land. Enquire
further about the mineral water : and take
notice of such plants as you meet with. I
am told that you are looked on in the Service
as exceeding faithful, valiant, diligent, gener-
ous, vigilant, observing, very knowing, and a
scholar. When you first took to this manner
of life, you cannot but remember that I caused
you to read all the sea-fights of note in
Plutarch : and, withal, gave you the description
of fortitude left by Aristotle. In places take
notice of the government of them, and the
eminent persons. The merciful providence of
God ever go with you, and direct and bless
you, and give you ever a grateful heart toward
Him. I send you Lucretius : and with it
Tully's Offices : 'tis as remarkable for its little
size as for the good matter contained in it,
and the authentic and classical Latin. I hope

you do not forget to carry a Greek Testament always to church : a man learns two things together, and profiteth doubly, in the language and the subject.   God send us to number our days, and to fit ourselves for a better world. Times look troublesome : but you have an honest and peaceable profession like myself, which may well employ you, and you have discretion to guide your words and actions. May God be reconciled to us, and give us grace to forsake our sins which set fire to all things.   You shall never want my daily prayers, and also frequent letters.'   And so on, through a delightful sheaf of letters to his two sons : and out of which a fine picture rises before us, both of Sir Thomas's own student life abroad, as well as of the footing on which the now famous physician and English author stood with his student and sailor sons.

You might read every word of Sir Thomas Browne's writings and never discover that a sword had been unsheathed or a shot fired in England all the time he was living and writing there.   It was the half-century of the terrible civil war for political and religious liberty : but Sir Thomas Browne would seem to have possessed all the political and religious liberty he needed. At any rate, he never took open part on either side in the great contest. Sir Thomas Browne was not made of the hot metal and the stern stuff of John Milton. All through those terrible years Browne lived securely in his laboratory, and in his library, and in his closet. Richard Baxter's *Autobiography* is as full of gunpowder as if it had been written in an army-chaplain's tent, as indeed it was. But both Bunyan's *Grace Abounding* and Browne's *Religio Medici* might have been written in the Bedford or Norwich of our own peaceful day. All men are not made to be soldiers and statesmen : and it is no man's duty to attempt to be what he was not made to be. Every man has his own talent, and his corresponding and consequent duty and obligation. And both Bunyan and Browne had their own talent, and their own consequent duty and obligation, just as Cromwell and Milton and Baxter had theirs. Enough, and more than enough, if it shall be said to them all on that day, Well done.

' My life,' says Sir Thomas, in opening one of the noblest chapters of his noblest book, ' is a miracle of thirty years, which to relate were not a history, but a piece of poetry ; and it would sound to common ears like a fable.'

Now, as all Sir Thomas's readers must know,
the most extraordinary criticisms and comments
have been made on those devout and thankful
words of his concerning himself.   Dr. Samuel
Johnson's were not common ears, but even he
comments on these beautiful words with a
wooden-headedness almost past belief.   For,
surely the thirty years of schoolboy, and
student, and opening professional life that
resulted in the production of such a masterpiece as the *Religio Medici* was a miracle both
of God's providence and God's grace, enough
to justify him who had experienced all that
in acknowledging it to God's glory and to the
unburdening of his own heart, so richly loaded
with God's benefits.   And, how a man of
Samuel Johnson's insight, good sense, and
pious feeling could have so missed the mark
in this case, I cannot understand.   All the
more that both the chapter so complained
about, and the whole book to which that
chapter belongs, are full of the same thankful,
devout, and adoring sentiment.   'The world
that I regard,' Sir Thomas proceeds, 'is myself.
Men that look upon my outside, and who
peruse only my conditions and my fortunes,
do err in my altitude.   There is surely a piece
of divinity in us all ; something that was

before the elements, and which owes no homage unto the sun.'   And again, 'We carry with us the wonders we seek without us.   There is all Africa and all its prodigies in us all.   We are that bold and adventurous piece of nature, which he that studies wisely learns, in a compendium, what others labour at in a divided piece and endless volume.'   And again, 'There is another way of God's providence full of meanders and labyrinths and obscure methods : that serpentine and crooked line : that cryptic and involved method of His providence which I have ever admired.   Surely there are in every man's life certain rubs, and doublings, and wrenches, which, well examined, do prove the pure hand of God.   And to be true, and to speak out my soul, when I survey the occurrences of my own life, and call into account the finger of God, I can perceive nothing but an abyss and a mass of mercies.   And those which others term crosses, and afflictions, and judgments, and misfortunes, to me they both appear, and in event have ever proved, the secret and dissembled favours of His affection.' And in the *Christian Morals* : 'Annihilate not the mercies of God by the oblivion of ingratitude.   Make not thy head a grave, but a repository of God's mercies.   Register not only strange, but all merciful occurrences. Let thy diaries stand thick with dutiful mementoes and asterisks of acknowledgment. And to be complete and to forget nothing, date not His mercy from thy nativity : look beyond this world, and before the era of Adam. And mark well the winding ways of providence. For that hand writes often by abbreviations, hieroglyphics, and short characters, which, like the laconism on Belshazzar's wall, are not to be made out but by a key from that Spirit that indited them.' And yet again, 'To thoughtful observers the whole world is one phylactery, and everything we see an item of the wisdom, and power, and goodness of God.' How any man, not to speak of one of the wisest and best of men, such as Samuel Johnson was, could read all that, and still stagger at Sir Thomas Browne holding himself to be a living miracle of the power, and the love, and the grace of God, passes my understanding.

We have seen in his own noble words how Sir Thomas Browne's life appeared to himself. Let us now look at how he appeared to other observing men. The Rev. John Whitefoot, the close and lifelong friend of Sir Thomas, has left us this lifelike portrait of the author of *Religio Medici*. 'For a character of his person, his complexion and his hair were answerable to his name, his stature was moderate, and his habit of body neither fat nor lean, but εὐσάρκος. In his habit of clothing he had an aversion to all finery, and affected plainness. He ever wore a cloke, or boots, when few others did. He kept himself always very warm, and thought it most safe so to do. The horizon of his understanding was much larger than the hemisphere of the world : all that was visible in the heavens he comprehended so well, that few that are under them knew so much. And of the earth he had such a minute and exact geographical knowledge as if he had been by divine providence ordained surveyor-general of the whole terrestrial orb and its products, minerals, plants, and animals. His memory, though not so eminent as that of Seneca or Scaliger, was capacious and tenacious, insomuch that he remembered all that was remarkable in any book he ever read. He had no despotical power over his affections and passions, that was a privilege of original perfection, but as large a political power over them as any stoic or man of his time, whereof he gave so great experiment that he hath very rarely been known to have been overpowered with any of them. His aspect and conversation were grave and sober ; there was never

to be seen in him anything trite or vulgar.
Parsimonious in nothing but his time, whereof
he made as much improvement, with as little
loss as any man in it, when he had any to spare
from his drudging practice, he was scarce
patient of any diversion from his study : so
impatient of sloth and idleness, that he would
say, he could not do nothing. He attended
the public service very constantly, when he was
not withheld by his practice. Never missed
the sacrament in his parish, if he were in town.
Read the best English sermons he could hear
of with liberal applause : and delighted not in
controversies.   His patience was founded upon
the Christian philosophy, and sound faith of
God's providence, and a meek and humble
submission thereto. I visited him near his
end, when he had not strength to hear or
speak much : and the last words I heard from
him were, besides some expressions of dearness,
that he did freely submit to the will of God :
being without fear.   He had oft triumphed
over the king of terrors in others, and given
him many repulses in the defence of patients ;
but when his own time came, he submitted
with a meek, rational, religious courage.'

Taking Sir Thomas Browne all in all, Tertullian, Sir Thomas's favourite Father, has

supplied us, as it seems to me, with his whole life and character in these so expressive and so comprehensive words of his, *Anima naturaliter Christiana*. In these three words, when well weighed and fully opened up, we have the whole author of the *Religio Medici*, the *Christian Morals*, and the *Letter to a Friend*. *Anima naturaliter Christiana*.

The *Religio Medici* was Sir Thomas Browne's first book, and it remains by far his best book. His other books acquire their value and take their rank just according to the degree of their ' affinity' to the *Religio Medici*. Sir Thomas Browne is at his best when he is most alone with himself. There is no subject that interests him so much as Sir Thomas Browne. And if you will forget yourself in Sir Thomas Browne, and in his conversations which he holds with himself, you will find a rare and an ever fresh delight in the *Religio Medici*. Sir Thomas is one of the greatest egotists of literature—to use a necessary but an unpopular and a misleading epithet. Hazlitt has it that there have only been but three perfect, absolute, and unapproached egotists in all literature—Cellini, Montaigne, and Wordsworth. But why that fine critic leaves out Sir

Thomas Browne, I cannot understand or accept. I always turn to Sir Thomas Browne, far more than to either of Hazlitt's canonised three, when I want to read what a great man has to tell me about himself : and in this case both a great and a good and a Christian man. And thus, whatever modification and adaptation may have been made in this masterpiece of his, in view of its publication, and after it was first published, the original essence, most genuine substance, and unique style of the book were all intended for its author's peculiar heart and private eye alone. And thus it is that we have a work of a simplicity and a sincerity that would have been impossible had its author in any part of his book sat down to compose for the public. Sir Thomas Browne lived so much within himself, that he was both secret writer and sole reader to himself. His great book is ' a private exercise directed solely,' as he himself says, ' to himself : it is a memorial addressed to himself rather than an example or a rule directed to any other man.' And it is only he who opens the *Religio Medici* honestly and easily believing that, and glad to have such a secret and sincere and devout book in his hand,—it is only he who will truly enjoy the book, and who will

gather the same gain out of it that its author
enjoyed and gained out of it himself.   In short,
the properly prepared and absolutely ingenuous
reader of the *Religio Medici* must be a second
Thomas Browne himself.

'I am a medical man,' says Sir Thomas, in
introducing himself to us, 'and this is my
religion. · I am a physician, and this is my
faith, and my morals, and my whole true and
proper life.   The scandal of my profession,
the natural course of my studies, and the
indifference of my behaviour and discourse
in matters of religion, might persuade the
world that I had no religion at all.   And yet,
in despite of all that, I dare, without usurpation,
assume the honourable style of a Christian.'
And if ever any man was a truly catholic
Christian, it was surely Sir Thomas Browne.
He does not unchurch or ostracise any other
man.   He does not stand at diameter and
sword's point with any other man ; no, not
even with his enemy.   He has never been able
to alienate or exasperate himself from any man
whatsoever because of a difference of an opinion.
He has never been angry with any man because
his judgment in matters of religion did not
agree with his.   In short he has no genius
for disputes about religion ; and he has often

felt it to be his best wisdom to decline all
such disputes.   When his head was greener
than it now is, he had a tendency to two or
three errors in religion, of which he proceeds
to set down the spiritual history.   But at no
time did he ever maintain his own opinions with
pertinacity : far less to inveigle or entangle any
other man's faith ; and thus they soon died
out, since they were only bare errors and
single lapses of his understanding, without a
joint depravity of his will.   The truth to
Sir Thomas Browne about all revealed religion
is this, which he sets forth in a deservedly
famous passage :—' Methinks there be not impossibilities enough in revealed religion for an
active faith.   I love to lose myself in a mystery,
and to pursue my reason to an *O altitudo !*
'Tis my solitary recreation to pose my apprehension with those involved enigmas and
riddles of the Trinity, with incarnation and
resurrection.   I can answer all the objections
of Satan and my rebellious reason with that
odd resolution I learned of Tertullian, *Certum
est quia impossibile est.*   I desire to exercise my
faith in the difficultest point ; for anything
else is not faith but persuasion.   I bless myself,
and am thankful that I never saw Christ nor
His disciples.   For then had my faith been

thrust upon me; nor should I have enjoyed
that greater blessing pronounced to all that
believe and saw not.   They only had the
advantage of a noble and a bold faith who
lived before the coming of Christ; and who,
upon obscure prophecies and mystical types,
could raise a belief and expect apparent impossibilities.   And since I was of understanding
enough to know that we know nothing, my
reason hath been more pliable to the will of
faith.   I am now content to understand a
mystery in an easy and Platonic way, and
without a demonstration and a rigid definition;
and thus I teach my haggard and unreclaimed
reason to stoop unto the lure of faith.'   The
unreclaimed reader who is not already allured
by these specimens need go no further in
Sir Thomas Browne's autobiographic book.
But he who feels the grace and the truth, the
power and the sweetness and the beauty of
such writing, will be glad to know that the
whole *Religio* is full of such things, and that
all this author's religious and moral writings
partake of the same truly Apostolic and truly
Platonic character.   In this noble temper, with
the richest mind, and clothed in a style that
entrances and captivates us, Sir Thomas proceeds to set forth his doctrine and experience

of God ; of God's providence ; of Holy
Scripture ; of nature and man ; of miracles
and oracles ; of the Holy Ghost and holy
angels ; of death ; and of heaven and hell.
And, especially, and with great fulness, and
victoriousness, and conclusiveness, he deals with
death.   We sometimes amuse ourselves by
making a selection of the two or three books
that we would take with us to prison or to a
desert island.   And one dying man here and
another there has already selected and set aside
the proper and most suitable books for his own
special deathbed.   'Read where I first cast my
anchor,' said John Knox to his wife, sitting
weeping at his bedside.   At which she opened
and read in the Gospel of John.   Sir Thomas
Browne is neither more nor less than the very
prose-laureate of death.   He writes as no
other man has ever written about death.   Death
is everywhere in all Sir Thomas Browne's
books.   And yet it may be said of them all,
that, like heaven itself, there is no death there.
Death is swallowed up in Sir Thomas Browne's
defiant faith that cannot, even in death,
get difficulties and impossibilities enough to
exercise itself upon.   O death, where is thy sting
to Rutherford, and Bunyan, and Baxter, and
Browne ; and to those who diet their imagina-

tions and their hearts day and night at such
heavenly tables ! But, if only to see how
great and good men differ, Spinoza has this
proposition and demonstration that a ' free man
thinks of nothing less than of death.' Browne
was a free man, but he thought of nothing more
than of death.   He was of Dante's mind—

The arrow seen beforehand slacks its flight.

The *Religio Medici* was Sir Thomas Browne's
first book, and the *Christian Morals* was his
last; but the two books are of such affinity to
one another that they will always be thought
of together. Only, the style that was already
almost too rich for our modern taste in the
Religio absolutely cloys and clogs us in the
Morals. The opening and the closing sentences
of this posthumous treatise will better convey
a taste of its strength and sweetness than any
estimate or eulogium of mine. ' Tread softly
and circumspectly in this funambulatory track,
and narrow path of goodness ; pursue virtue
virtuously : leaven not good actions, nor
render virtue disputable. Stain not fair acts
with foul intentions ; maim not uprightness
by halting concomitances, nor circumstantially
deprave substantial goodness. Consider where-
about thou art in Cebes' table, or that old

philosophical pinax of the life of man : whether
thou art yet in the road .of uncertainties;
whether thou hast yet entered the narrow gate,
got up the hill and asperous way which leadeth
unto the house of sanity ; or taken that purify-
ing potion from the hand of sincere erudi-
tion, which may send thee clear and pure away
unto a virtuous and happy life.'   And having
taken his reader up through a virtuous life,
Sir Thomas thus parts with him at its close :
' Lastly, if length of days be thy portion, make
it not thy expectation.   Reckon not upon
long life ; think every day thy last.   And
since there is something in us that will still
live on, join both lives together, and live in
one but for the other.   And if any hath been
so happy as personally to understand Christian
annihilation, ecstasy, exaltation, transformation,
the kiss of the spouse, and ingression into
the divine shadow, according to mystical
theology, they have already had an handsome
anticipation of heaven : the world is in a
manner over, and the earth in ashes unto
them.'   ' Prose,' says Friswell, ' that with very
little transposition, might make verse quite
worthy of Shakespeare himself.'

The *Letter to a Friend* is an account of

the swift and inevitable deathbed of one of Sir Thomas's patients : a young man who died of a deceitful but a galloping consumption. There is enough of old medical observation and opening science in the *Letter*, as well as of sweet old literature, and still sweeter old religion, to make it a classic to every well-read doctor in the language. 'To be dissolved and to be with Christ was his dying ditty. He esteemed it enough to approach the years of his Saviour, who so ordered His own human state, as not to be old upon earth. He that early arriveth into the parts and prudence of age is happily old without the uncomfortable attendants of it. And 'tis superfluous to live unto grey hairs, when in a precocious temper we anticipate the virtues of them. In brief, he cannot be accounted young who outliveth the old man.' Let all young medical students have by heart Sir Thomas Browne's incomparable English, and wisdom, and piety in his *Letter to a Friend upon the occasion of the death of his intimate Friend.* 'This unique morsel of literature' as Walter Pater calls it.

The *Vulgar Errors*, it must be confessed, is neither very inviting, nor very rewarding to ordinary readers nowadays. And that big book will only be persevered in to the end by those readers

to whom everything that Sir Thomas Browne
has written is of a rare interest and profit.   The
full title of this now completely antiquated
and wholly forgotten treatise is this, ' *Pseudodoxia Epidemica*, or Enquiries into very many
received Tenets and commonly presumed
Truths, which examined prove but Vulgar
and Common Errors.'   The First Book of the
Pseudodoxia is general and philosophical ; the
Second Book treats of popular and received
tenets concerning mineral and vegetable bodies ;
the Third, of popular and received tenets concerning animals ; the Fourth, of man ; the
Fifth, of many things questionable as they are
commonly described in pictures, etc. ; and the
Sixth, of popular and received tenets, cosmo-
graphical, geographical, and historical ; and the
Seventh, of popular and received truth, some
historical, and some deduced from Holy
Scripture.   The Introductory Book contains
the best analysis and exposition of the famous
Baconian Idols that has ever been written.
That Book of the *Pseudodoxia* is full of the pro-
foundest philosophical principles set forth in the
stateliest English.   The students of Whately
and Mill, as well as of Bacon, will greatly enjoy
this part of the *Pseudodoxia*.   *The Grammar
of Assent*, also, would seem to have had some of

its deepest roots in the same powerful, original, and suggestive Book.   For its day the *Pseudo-doxia* is a perfect encyclopædia of scientific, and historical, and literary, and even Biblical criticism : the *Pseudodoxia* and the *Miscellany Tracts* taken together.   Some of the most powerful passages that ever fell from Sir Thomas Browne's pen are to be come upon in the Introduction to the *Pseudodoxia*.   And, with all our immense advances in method and in discipline : in observation and in discovery : no true student of nature and of man can afford to neglect the extraordinary catalogue of things which are so characteristically treated of in Sir Thomas Browne's great, if, nowadays, out-grown book.   For one thing, and that surely not a small thing, we see on every page of the *Pseudodoxia* the labour, as Dr. Johnson so truly says, that its author was always willing to pay for the truth.   And, as Sir Thomas says himself, a work of this nature is not to be performed upon one leg, or without the smell of oil, if it is to be duly and deservedly handled.   It must be left to men of learning and of science to say how far Sir Thomas has duly and deservedly handled the immense task he undertook in this book.   But I, for one, have read this great treatise with a

true pride, in seeing so much hard work so
liberally laid out according to the best light
allowed its author in that day.   As Dr. Johnson
has said of it, 'The mistakes that the author
committed in the *Pseudodoxia* were not committed by idleness or negligence, but only for
want of the philosophy of Boyle and Newton.'
Who, then, will gird up his loins in our
enlightened day to give us a new *Pseudodoxia*
after the philosophy of Bacon and Boyle and
Newton and Ewald and Darwin ?   And after
Sir Thomas's own philosophy, which he thus
sets forth before himself in this and in all his
other studies :   'We are not magisterial in
opinions, nor have we dictator-like obtruded our
conceptions : but, in the humility of inquiries
or disquisitions, have only proposed them to
more ocular discerners.   And we shall so far
encourage contradiction as to promise no disturb-
ance, or re-oppose any pen, that shall failaciously
or captiously refute us.   And shall only take
notice of such whose experimental and judicious
knowledge shall be employed, not to traduce or
extenuate, but to explain and dilucidate, to
add and ampliate, according to the laudable
custom of the ancients in their sober promo-
tions of learning.   Unto whom, notwithstanding, we shall not contentiously rejoin, or only

to justify our own, but to applaud or confirm
his maturer assertions; and shall confer what
is in us unto his name and honour; ready,
for our part, to be swallowed up in any
worthy enlarger: as having our aid, if any
way, or under any name, we may obtain a
work, so much desired, and yet desiderated, of
truth.' Shall this Association, I wonder, raise
up from among its members, such a worthy
successor and enlarger of Sir Thomas Browne?

The title, at least, of the *Urn-Burial* is more
familiar to the most of us than that of the
Pseudodoxia. It was the chance discovery of
some ancient urns in Norfolk that furnished
Sir Thomas with the occasion to write his
Hydriotaphia. And that classical book is only
another illustration of his enormous reading,
ready memory, and intense interest in everything that touches on the nature of man, and
on his beliefs, habits, and hopes in all ages of
his existence on this earth. And the eloquence
and splendour of this wonderful piece is as
arresting to the student of style as its immense
information is to the scholar and the antiquarian. 'The conclusion of the essay on Urn-
Burial,' says Carlyle, 'is absolutely beautiful:
a still elegiac mood, so soft, so deep, so solemn
and tender, like the song of some departed

saint—an echo of deepest meaning from the great and mighty Nations of the Dead. Sir Thomas Browne must have been a good man.'

The Garden of Cyrus is past all description of mine. *The Garden of Cyrus* must be read. It is an extravagant sport of a scholar of the first rank and a genius of the first water. ' We write no herbal,' he begins, and neither he does. And after the most fantastical prose-poem surely that ever was written, he as fantastically winds up at midnight with this : ' To keep our eyes longer open were but to act our anti- podes. The huntsmen are up in America, and they are already past their first sleep in Persia.' At which Coleridge must incontinently whip out his pencil till we have this note of his on the margin : ' What life ! what fancy ! what whim- sicality ! Was ever such a reason given for leav- ing one's book and going to bed as this, that they are already past their first sleep in Persia, and that the huntsmen are up in America ? '

Sir Thomas Browne has had many admirers, and his greatest admirers are to be found among our foremost men. He has had Samuel Johnson among his greatest admirers, and Coleridge, and Carlyle, and Hazlitt, and Lytton, and Walter Pater, and Leslie Stephen, and Professor Saintsbury ; than whom no one of

them all has written better on Browne. And he
has had princely editors and annotators in Simon
Wilkin, and Dr. Greenhill, and Dr. Lloyd
Roberts. I must leave it to those eminent
men to speak to you with all their authority
about Sir Thomas Browne's ten talents : his
unique natural endowments, his universal
scholarship, his philosophical depth, ' his
melancholy yet affable irony,' his professional
and scientific attainments, and his absolutely
classical English style. And I shall give
myself up, in ending this discourse, to what
is of much more importance to him and to us
all, than all these things taken together,—for
Sir Thomas Browne was a believing man, and
a man of unfainting and unrelaxing prayer. At
the same time, and assuming, as he does, and
that without usurpation, as he says, the style
of a Christian, he is in reality a Theist rather
than a Christian : he is a moral and a religious writer rather than an evangelical and
an experimental writer. And in saying this,
I do not forget his confession of his faith.
' But to difference myself nearer,' he says,
and ' to draw into a lesser circle, there is
no Church whose every part so squares unto
my conscience : whose Articles, Constitutions,
and Customs seem so consonant unto reason,

and as it were framed to my particular Devotion, as this whereof I hold my Belief, the
Church of England : to whose faith I am a
sworn subject, and therefore in a double
Obligation subscribe unto her Articles, and
endeavour to observe her Constitutions.' The
author of the *Religio Medici* never writes a
line out of joint, or out of tone or temper,
with that subscription. At the same time,
his very best writings fall far short of the
best writings of the Church of England.
Pater, in his fine paper, says that 'Sir Thomas
Browne is occupied with religion first and last
in all he writes, scarcely less so than Hooker
himself,' and that is the simple truth. Still, if
the whole truth is to be told to those who will
not make an unfair use of it, Richard Hooker's
religion is the whole Christian religion, in all
its height and depth, and grace and truth, and
doctrinal and evangelical fulness : all of which
can never be said of Sir Thomas Browne. I
can well imagine Sir Thomas Browne recreat-
ing himself, and that with an immense delecta-
tion, over Hooker's superb First Book. How
I wish that I could say as much about the
central six chapters of Hooker's masterly
Fifth Book : as also about his evangelical and
immortal *Discourse of Justification* ! A well-

read friend of mine suddenly said to me in a conversation we were holding the other day about Sir Thomas Browne's religion, 'The truth is,' he said, 'Browne was nothing short of a Pelagian, and that largely accounts for his popularity on the Continent of his day.' That was a stroke of true criticism. And Sir Thomas's own Tertullian has the same thing in that most comprehensive and conclusive phrase of his : *anima naturaliter Christiana.* But, that being admitted and accepted, which must be admitted and accepted in the interests of the truth ; this also must still more be proclaimed, admitted, and accepted, that when he comes to God, and to Holy Scripture, and to prayer, and to immortality, Sir Thomas Browne is a very prince of believers. In all these great regions of things Sir Thomas Browne's faith has a height and a depth, a strength and a sweep, that all combine together to place him in the very foremost rank of our most classical writers on natural and revealed religion. Hooker himself in some respects gives place to Sir Thomas Browne.

'I had rather believe all the fables in the Legend, and the Talmud, and the Alcoran, than that this universal frame is without a mind : and therefore, God never

wrought miracles to convince atheism, because
His ordinary works convince it. It is true,
that a little philosophy inclineth man's mind
to atheism, but depth in philosophy bringeth
men's minds about to religion.' The old
proverb, *Ubi tres medici, duo athei*, cast an
opprobrium on the medical profession that
can never have been just. At the same time,
that proverb may be taken as proving
how little true philosophy there must have
been at one time among the medical men of
Europe. Whereas, in Sir Thomas Browne
at any rate, his philosophy was of such a
depth that to him, as he repeatedly tells us,
atheism, or anything like atheism, had always
been absolutely impossible. 'Mine is that
mystical philosophy, from whence no true
scholar becomes an atheist, but from the visible
effects of nature, grows up a real divine, and
beholds, not in a dream, as Ezekiel, but in an
ocular and visible object, the types of his resurrection.' Nor can he dedicate his *Urn-Burial*
to his worthy and honoured friend without
counselling him to 'run up his thoughts upon
the Ancient of Days, the antiquary's truest
object'; so continually does Browne's imagination in all his books pierce into and terminate
upon Divine Persons and upon unseen and

eternal things. In his rare imagination, Sir
Thomas Browne had the original root of a
truly refining, ennobling, and sanctifying faith
planted in his heart by the hand of Nature her-
self. No man, indeed, in the nature of things,
can be a believing Christian man without imagination. A believing and a heavenly-minded man
may have a fine imagination without knowing
that he has it. He may have it without knowing or admitting the name of it. He may have
it, and may be constantly employing it, without being taught, and without discovering, how
most nobly and most fruitfully to employ it.
Not Shakespeare ; not Milton ; not Scott :
scarcely Tennyson or Browning themselves,
knew how best to employ their imagination.
Only Dante and Behmen of all the foremost
sons of men. Only they two turned all their
splendid and unapproached imagination to the
true, and full, and final Objects of Christian
faith. Only to them two was their magnificent
imagination the substance of things hoped for,
and the evidence of things not seen. And
though the *Religio* does not at all rank with
the *Commedia* and the *Aurora*, at the same
time, it springs up from, and it is strengthened
and sweetened by the same intellectual and
spiritual root. Up through all 'the weeds and

tares of his brain,' as Sir Thomas himself calls them, his imagination and his faith shot, and sprang, and spread, till they covered with their finest fruits his whole mind, and heart, and life.

Sir Thomas Browne was a noble illustration of Bacon's noble law.   For Sir Thomas carried all his studies, experiments, and operations to such a depth in his own mind, and heart, and imagination, that he was able to testify to all his fellow-physicians that he who studies man and medicine deeply enough will meet with as many intellectual, and scientific, and religious adventures every day as any traveller will meet with in Africa itself.   As a living man of genius in the medical profession, Dr. George Gould, has it in that wonderful Behmenite and Darwinian book of his, *The Meaning and the Method of Life*, 'A healing and a knitting wound,' he argues, 'is quite as good a proof of God as a sensible mind would desire.'   This was Sir Thomas Browne's wise, and deep, and devout mind in all parts of his professional and personal life.   And he was man enough, and a man of true science and of true religion enough, to warn his brethren against those 'academical reservations' to which their strong intellectual and professional pride, and their too weak faith

and courage, continually tempted them. Nor
has he, for his part, any clinical reservations in
religion either, as so many of his brethren have.
'I cannot go to cure the body of my patient,'
he protests, 'but I forget my profession and call
unto God for his soul.' To call Sir Thomas
Browne sceptical, as has been a caprice and a
fashion among his merely literary admirers :
and to say it, till it is taken for granted, that he
is an English Montaigne : all that is an abuse
of language. It is, to all but a small and select
circle of writers and readers, utterly misleading
and essentially untrue. And, besides, it is right
in the teeth of Sir Thomas's own emphatic, and
repeated, and indignant denial and repudiation
of Montaigne. Montaigne, with all his fascina-
tions for literary men, and they are great ; and
with all his services to them, and they are not
small ; is both an immoral and an unbelieving
writer. Whereas, Sir Thomas Browne never
wrote a single line, even in his greenest studies,
that on his deathbed he desired to blot out.
A purer, a humbler, a more devout and de-
tached hand never put English pen to paper
than was the hand of Sir Thomas Browne.
And, if ever in his greener days he had a
doubt about any truth of natural or of revealed
religion, he tells us that he had fought down

every such doubt in his closet and on his knees.

I will not profanely paraphrase, or in any way water down the strong words in which Sir Thomas Browne writes to himself in his secret papers about prayer. All that has been said about this very remarkable man only makes what we are now to read all the more remarkable and memorable. All Sir Thomas Browne's readers owe an immense debt to Simon Wilkin; and for nothing more than for rescuing for us these golden words of this man of God. 'They were not,' says Wilkin, 'intended by Browne for the perusal of his son, as so many of his private papers were, or of any one else.' And hence their priceless value.

' To be sure that no day pass without calling upon God in a solemn, fervent prayer, seven times within the compass thereof. That is, in the morning, and at night, and five times between. Taken up long ago from the example of David and Daniel, and a compunction and shame that I had omitted it so long, when I heedfully read of the custom of the Mahometans to pray five times in the day.

' To pray and magnify God in the night, and in my dark bed, when I cannot sleep ; to

have short ejaculations whenever I awake, and
when the four o'clock bell awakens me ; or on
my first discovery of the light, to say this
collect of our liturgy, Eternal God, who hast
safely brought me to the beginning of this
day. . . .

'To pray in all places where privacy in-
viteth : in any house, highway, or street : and
to know no street or passage in this city which
may not witness that I have not forgot God
and my Saviour in it ; and that no parish or
town where I have been may not say the like.

'To take occasion of praying upon the
sight of any church which I see or pass by as I
ride about.

'Since the necessities of the sick, and un-
avoidable diversions of my profession, keep
me often from church ; yet to take all possible
care that I might never miss sacraments upon
their accustomed days.

'To pray daily and particularly for sick
patients, and in general for others, wheresoever,
howsoever, under whose care soever ; and at
the entrance into the house of the sick, to say,
The peace and mercy of God be in this place.

'After a sermon, to make a thanksgiving,
and desire a blessing, and to pray for the
minister.

'In tempestuous weather, lightning, and thunder, either night or day, to pray for God's merciful protection upon all men, and His mercy upon their souls, bodies, and goods.

'Upon sight of beautiful persons, to bless God for His creatures : to pray for the beauty of their souls, and that He would enrich them with inward grace to be answerable to the outward. Upon sight of deformed persons, to pray Him to send them inward graces, and to enrich their souls, and give them the beauty of the resurrection.'

'But the greatest of these is charity.' Charity is greater than great talents. Charity is greater than great industry. Charity is greater than great learning and great literature. Charity is greater than great faith. Charity is greater than great prayer. For charity is nothing less than the Divine Nature Itself in the heart of man. In all English literature two books stand out beside one another and are alone in this supreme respect of charity : William Law's *Spirit of Love*, and Sir Thomas Browne's *Religio Medici*.

SELECTED PASSAGES

SELECTED PASSAGES

I HAVE ever endeavoured to nourish the merciful disposition and humane inclination I borrowed from my parents, and regulate it to the written and prescribed laws of charity; and if I hold the true anatomy of myself, I am delineated and naturally framed to such a piece of virtue. For I am of a constitution so general that it comports and sympathiseth with all things; I have no antipathy, or rather idiosyncrasy, in diet, humour, air, anything. I wonder not at the French for their dishes of frogs, snails, and toadstools; nor at the Jews for locusts and grasshoppers; but being amongst them, make them my common viands; and I find them agree with my stomach as well as theirs. I could digest a salad gathered in a churchyard as well as in a garden. I cannot start at the presence of a serpent, scorpion, lizard, or salamander: at the sight of a toad or viper I find in me no desire to take up a stone to destroy them. I feel not in myself those common antipathies that I can discover in others. Those national repugnances do not touch me, nor do I behold with prejudice the French, Italian, Spaniard, and Dutch : but where I find their actions in balance with my countrymen's, I honour, love, and embrace them in the same degree. I was born in the eighth climate, but seem to be framed and constellated unto all. I am no plant that will not prosper out of a garden : all places, all airs make unto me one country—I am in England everywhere, and under any meridian. I have been shipwrecked, yet am not enemy with the sea or winds. I can study, play, or sleep in a tempest. In brief, I am averse from nothing : my conscience would give me the lie if I should absolutely detest or hate any essence but the devil ; or so at least abhor anything, but that we might come to composition.

I am, I confess, naturally inclined to that which misguided zeal terms superstition : my common conversation I do acknowledge austere, my behaviour full of rigour, sometimes not without morosity ; yet at my devotion I love to use the civility of my knee, my hat, and hand, with all those outward and sensible motions which may express or promote my invisible devotion. I should violate my own arm rather than a church, nor willingly deface the name of saint or martyr. At the sight of a cross or crucifix I can dispense with my hat, but scarce with the thought or memory of my Saviour : I cannot laugh at, but rather pity the fruitless journeys of pilgrims, or contemn the miserable condition of friars ; for though misplaced in circumstances, there is something in it of devotion. I could never hear the Ave Maria bell without an elevation, or think it a sufficient warrant, because they erred in one circumstance, for me to err in all, that is, in silence and dumb contempt; whilst therefore they direct their devotions to her, I offer mine to God, and rectify the errors of their prayers, by rightly ordering mine own. At a solemn procession I have wept abundantly, while my consorts, blind with opposition and prejudice, have fallen into an excess of scorn and laughter. There are, questionless, both in Greek, Roman, and African churches, solemnities and ceremonies, whereof the wiser zeals do make a Christian use, and stand condemned by us, not as evil in themselves, but as allurements and baits of superstition to those vulgar heads that look asquint on the face of truth, and those unstable judgments that cannot consist in the narrow point and centre of virtue without a reel or stagger to the circumference.

As for those wingy mysteries in divinity, and airy subtleties in religion, which have unhinged the brains of better heads, they never stretched the *pia mater* of mine. Methinks there be not impossibilities enough in religion for an active faith; the deepest mysteries ours contains, have not only been illustrated, but maintained by syllogism, and the rule of reason. I love to lose myself in a mystery, to pursue my reason to an *O altitudo!* It is my solitary recreation to pose my apprehension with those involved enigmas and riddles of the Trinity, with incarnation and resurrection. I can answer all the objections of Satan and my rebellious reason, with that odd resolution I learned of Tertullian, *Certum est quia impossibile est.* I desire to exercise my faith in the difficultest point; for to credit ordinary and visible objects, is not faith, but persuasion. Some believe the better for seeing Christ's sepulchre; and when they have seen the Red Sea, doubt not of the miracle. Now, contrarily, I bless myself, and am thankful that I lived not in the days of miracles; that I never saw Christ

nor His disciples.   I would not have been one
of those Israelites that passed the Red Sea, nor
one of Christ's patients on whom He wrought
His wonders ; then had my faith been thrust
upon me, nor should I enjoy that greater
blessing pronounced to all that believe and
saw not.   It is an easy and necessary belief, to
credit what our eye and sense hath examined :
I believe He was dead and buried, and rose
again ; and desire to see Him in His glory,
rather than to contemplate Him in His cenotaph
or sepulchre.   Nor is this much to believe ;
as we have reason, we owe this faith unto
history.   They only had the advantage of a
bold and noble faith, who lived before His
coming, who upon obscure prophecies and
mystical types could raise a belief and expect
apparent impossibilities.

Now for my life, it is a miracle of thirty
years, which to relate were not a history but a
piece of poetry, and would sound to common
ears like a fable ; for the world, I count it not
an inn but an hospital ; and a place not to
live, but to die in.   The world that I regard is
myself ; it is the microcosm of my own frame
that I cast mine eye on ; for the other, I use it
but like my globe, and turn it round sometimes
for my recreation.   Men that look upon my

outside, perusing only my condition and fortunes, do err in my altitude, for I am above Atlas's shoulders. The earth is a point, not only in respect of the heavens above us, but of that heavenly and celestial part within us ; that mass of flesh that circumscribes me limits not my mind ; that surface that tells the heaven it hath an end cannot persuade me I have any. I take my circle to be above three hundred and sixty. Though the number of the arc do measure my body it comprehendeth not my mind. Whilst I study to find how I am a microcosm, or little world, I find myself something more than the great. There is surely a piece of divinity in us, something that was before the elements, and owes no homage unto the sun. Nature tells me I am the image of God, as well as Scripture. He that understands not thus much hath not his introduction, or first lesson, and is yet to begin the alphabet of man.

ON GOD

In my solitary and retired imagination, I remember I am not alone, and therefore forget not to contemplate Him and His attributes who is ever with me, especially those two

mighty ones, His wisdom and eternity; with
the one I recreate, with the other I confound
my understanding : for who can speak of
eternity without a solecism, or think thereof
without an ecstasy? Time we may comprehend. It is but five days older than ourselves,
and hath the same horoscope with the world ;
but to retire so far back as to apprehend a
beginning, to give such an infinite start for-
wards as to conceive an end in an essence that
we affirm hath neither the one nor the other,
it puts my reason to St. Paul's sanctuary.
My philosophy dares not say the angels can
do it ; God hath not made a creature that
can comprehend Him ; it is a privilege of His
own nature. 'I am that I am,' was His own
definition unto Moses; and it was a short one,
to confound mortality, that durst question God,
or ask Him what He was ; indeed He only is ;
all others have been and shall be. But in
eternity there is no distinction of tenses ; and
therefore that terrible term, predestination,
which hath troubled so many weak heads to
conceive, and the wisest to explain, is in respect
to God no prescious determination of our
estates to come, but a definitive blast of His
will already fulfilled, and at the instant that
He first decreed it ; for to His eternity which is

indivisible, and altogether, the last trump is already sounded, the reprobates in the flame, and the blessed in Abraham's bosom.

That other attribute wherewith I recreate my devotion is His wisdom, in which I am happy ; and for the contemplation of this only, do not repent me that I was bred in the way of study : the advantage I have of the vulgar, with the content and happiness I conceive therein, is an ample recompense for all my endeavours, in what part of knowledge soever, Wisdom is His most beauteous attribute ; no man can attain unto it : yet Solomon pleased God when he desired it. He is wise, because He knows all things ; and He knoweth all things, because He made them all : but His greatest knowledge is in comprehending that He made not, that is, Himself. And this is also the greatest knowledge in man. For this do I honour my own profession, and embrace the counsel even of the devil himself : had he read such a lecture in paradise, as he did at Delphos, we had better known ourselves ; nor had we stood in fear to know him. I know God is wise in all, wonderful in what we conceive, but far more in what we comprehend not ; for we behold Him but asquint upon reflex or shadow ; our understanding is dimmer

than Moses' eye; we are ignorant of the back
parts or lower side of His divinity; therefore to pry into the maze of His counsels, is
not only folly in man, but presumption even in
angels; like us, they are His servants, not His
senators; He holds no counsel, but that mystical
one of the Trinity, wherein though there be
three persons, there is but one mind that de-
crees without contradiction: nor needs He any;
His actions are not begot with deliberation, His
wisdom naturally knows what is best; His in-
tellect stands ready fraught with the superlative
and purest ideas of goodness; consultation
and election, which are two motions in us,
make but one in Him; His action springing
from His power, at the first touch of His will.
These are contemplations metaphysical: my
humble speculations have another method, and
are content to trace and discover those expressions he hath left in His creatures, and the
obvious effects of nature; there is no danger
to profound these mysteries, no *sanctum sanc-
torum* in philosophy: the world was made to
be inhabited by beasts; but studied and con-
templated by man: it is the debt of our
reason we owe unto God, and the homage
we pay for not being beasts; without this,
the world is still as though it had not been,

or as it was before the sixth day, when as yet
there was not a creature that could conceive, or
say there was a world.   The wisdom of God
receives small honour from those vulgar heads
that rudely stare about, and with a gross
rusticity admire His works; those highly
magnify Him, whose judicious inquiry into His
acts, and deliberate research into His creatures,
return the duty of a devout and learned admiration.   Therefore

> Search where thou wilt, and let thy reason go
> To ransom truth even to th' abyss below;
> Rally the scattered causes: and that line
> Which nature twists, be able to untwine;
> It is thy Maker's will, for unto none,
> But unto reason can He e'er be known.

ON THE SPIRIT OF GOD

However, I am sure there is a common
spirit that plays within us, yet makes no part
in us; and that is the Spirit of God, the fire
and scintillation of that noble and mighty
essence, which is the life and radical heat of
spirits, and those essences that know not the
virtue of the sun, a fire quite contrary to the
fire of hell.   This is that gentle heat that
brooded on the waters, and in six days hatched

the world; this is that irradiation that dispels
the mists of hell, the clouds of horror, fear,
sorrow, despair; and preserves the region of
the mind in serenity. Whatsoever feels not
the warm gale and gentle ventilation of this
spirit (though I feel his pulse), I dare not say
he lives; for truly without this, to me there
is no heat under the tropic; nor any light,
though I dwelt in the body of the sun.

> As when the labouring sun hath wrought his track
> Up to the top of lofty Cancer's back,
> The icy ocean cracks, the frozen pole
> Thaws with the heat of the celestial coal;
> So when Thy absent beams begin t'impart
> Again a solstice on my frozen heart,
> My winter's o'er, my drooping spirits sing,
> And every part revives into a spring.
> But if Thy quick'ning beams awhile decline,
> And with their light bless not this orb of mine,
> A chilly frost surpriseth every member,
> And in the midst of June I feel December.
> O how this earthly temper doth debase
> The noble soul, in this her humble place!
> Whose wingy nature ever doth aspire
> To reach that place whence first it took its fire.
> These flames I feel, which in my heart do dwell,
> Are not Thy beams, but take their fire from hell.
> O quench them all, and let Thy light divine,
> Be as the sun to this poor orb of mine:
> And to Thy sacred spirit convert those fires,
> Whose earthly fumes choke my devout aspires.

ON THE MERCY OF GOD

The great attribute of God—His mercy;
and, to be true, and speak my soul, when I
survey the occurrences of my life, and call
into account the finger of God, I can perceive
nothing but an abyss and mass of mercies,
either in general to mankind, or in particular
to myself: and whether out of the prejudice
of my affection, or an inverting and partial
conceit of His mercies, I know not ; but those
which others term crosses, afflictions, judgments, misfortunes, to me, who inquire further
into them than their visible effects, they both
appear, and in event have ever proved, the
secret and dissembled favours of His affection.
It is a singular piece of wisdom to apprehend
truly, and without passion, the works of God ;
and so well to distinguish His justice from His
mercy, as not to miscall those noble attributes;
yet it is likewise an honest piece of logic, so to
dispute and argue the proceedings of God, as
to distinguish even His judgments into mercies.
For God is merciful unto all, because better to
the worst than the best deserve ; and to say He
punisheth none in this world, though it be a
paradox, is no absurdity.   To one that hath
committed murder, if the judge should only

ordain a fine, it were a madness to call this
a punishment, and to repine at the sentence
rather than admire the clemency of the judge.
Thus our offences being mortal, and deserving
not only death, but damnation ; if the goodness of God be content to traverse and pass
them over with a loss, misfortune, or disease,
what frenzy were it to term this a punishment,
rather than an extremity of mercy ; and to
groan under the rod of His judgments, rather
than admire the sceptre of His mercies !

ON THE HOLY SCRIPTURES

Such I do believe the holy Scriptures ; yet
were it of man, I could not choose but say,
it was the singularest, and superlative piece
that hath been extant since the creation ; were
I a Pagan, I should not refrain the lecture of
it, and cannot but commend the judgment
of Ptolemy, that thought not his library complete without it. The Alcoran of the Turks
(I speak without prejudice) is an ill-composed
piece, containing in it vain and ridiculous errors
in philosophy, impossibilities, fictions, and
vanities beyond laughter, maintained by evident
and open sophisms, the policy of ignorance,
deposition of universities, and banishment of

learning, that hath gotten foot by arms and violence ; this, without a blow, hath disseminated itself through the whole earth. It is not unremarkable what Philo first observed, that the law of Moses continued two thousand years without the least alteration ; whereas, we see the laws of other commonwealths do alter with occasions; and even those that pretend their original from some divinity, to have vanished without trace or memory. I believe, besides Zoroaster, there were divers that wrote before Moses, who, notwithstanding, have suffered the common fate of time. Men's works have an age like themselves, and though they outlive their authors, yet have they a stint and period to their duration. This only is a work too hard for the teeth of time, and cannot perish but in the general flames, when all things shall confess their ashes.

Rest not in the high-strained paradoxes of old philosophy, supported by naked reason, and the reward of mortal felicity ; but labour in the ethics of faith, built upon heavenly assistance, and the happiness of both beings. Understand the rules, but swear not unto the doctrines of Zeno or Epicurus. Look beyond Antonius, and terminate not thy morals in Seneca or Epictetus. Let not the twelve but the two tables be thy law: let Pythagoras be thy remembrancer, not thy textuary and final instructor: and learn the vanity of the world, rather from Solomon than Phocylydes. Sleep not in the dogmas of the Peripatus, Academy, or Porticus. Be a moralist of the mount, an Epictetus in the faith, and christianise thy notions.

ON PROVIDENCE

And truly there goes a great deal of providence to produce a man's life unto threescore; there is more required than an able temper for those years; though the radical humour contain in it sufficient oil for seventy, yet I perceive in some it gives no light past thirty: men assign not all the causes of long life, that write whole books thereof. They that found themselves on the radical balsam, or vital sulphur of the parts, determine not why Abel lived not so long as Adam. There is therefore a secret glome or bottom of our days; it was his wisdom to determine them, but his perpetual and waking providence that fulfils and accomplishes them; wherein the spirits, ourselves, and all the creatures of God in a secret and disputed way do execute His will. Let them not, therefore, complain of immaturity that die about thirty: they fall but like the whole world, whose solid and well-composed substance must not expect the duration and period of its constitution ; when all things are completed in it, its age is accomplished ; and the last and general fever may as naturally destroy it before six thousand, as me before forty. There is therefore some other hand that twines the thread of life than that of nature ; we are not only ignorant in antipathies and occult qualities ; our ends are as obscure as our beginnings ; the line of our days is drawn by night, and the various effects therein by a pencil that is invisible ; wherein, though we confess our ignorance, I am sure we do not err if we say it is the hand of God.

ON ANGELS

Therefore for spirits, I am so far from denying their existence, that I could easily believe, that not only whole countries, but particular persons have their tutelary and guardian angels ; it is not a new opinion of the Church of Rome, but an old one of Pythagoras and Plato : there is no heresy in it, and if not manifestly defined in Scripture, yet is an opinion of a good and wholesome use in the

course and actions of a man's life, and would
serve as an hypothesis to solve many doubts,
whereof common philosophy affordeth no solu-
tion. Now, if you demand my opinion and
metaphysics of their natures, I confess them
very shallow, most of them in a negative way,
like that of God; or in a comparative, between
ourselves and fellow-creatures; for there is
in this universe a stair, or manifest scale of
creatures, rising not disorderly or in confusion,
but with a comely method and proportion.
Between creatures of mere existence and things
of life, there is a large disproportion of nature;
between plants and animals and creatures of
sense, a wider difference; between them and
man, a far greater: and if the proportion hold
on, between man and angels there should be
yet a greater. We do not comprehend their
natures, who retain the first definition of
Porphyry, and distinguish them from ourselves
by immortality; for before his fall, it is
thought man also was immortal; yet must we
needs affirm that he had a different essence
from the angels; having, therefore, no certain
knowledge of their natures, it is no bad method
of the schools, whatsoever perfection we find
obscurely in ourselves, in a more complete and
absolute way to ascribe unto them. I believe

they have an extemporary knowledge, and upon
the first motion of their reason do what we
cannot without study or deliberation ; that
they know things by their forms, and define
by specifical difference what we describe by
accidents and properties ; and therefore pro-
babilities to us may be demonstrations unto
them : that they have knowledge not only of
the specifical, but numerical forms of indivi-
duals, and understand by what reserved difference each single hypostasis (besides the relation
to its species) becomes its numerical self.
That as the soul hath power to move the body
it informs, so there is a faculty to move any,
though inform none ; ours upon restraint of
time, place, and distance ; but that invisible
hand that conveyed Habakkuk to the lions'
den, or Philip to Azotos, infringeth this rule,
and hath a secret conveyance, wherewith mortality is not acquainted.   If they have that
intuitive knowledge, whereby, as in reflection,
they behold the thoughts of one another, I cannot peremptorily deny but they know a great
part of ours.   They that to refute the invoca-
tion of saints have denied that they have any
knowledge of our affairs below, have proceeded
too far, and must pardon my opinion, till I can
thoroughly answer that piece of Scripture, ' At

the conversion of a sinner the angels in heaven
rejoice.' I cannot with those in that great
Father securely interpret the work of the first
day, *fiat lux*, to the creation of angels, though
I confess there is not any creature that hath so
near a glimpse of their nature, as light in the
sun and elements. We style it a bare accident,
but where it subsists alone it is a spiritual substance, and may be an angel : in brief, conceive
light invisible, and that is a spirit.

I could never pass that sentence of Paracelsus,
without an asterisk, or annotation ; *Ascendens
constellatum multa revelat, quærentibus magnalia
naturæ*, i.e. *opera Dei*. I do think that many
mysteries ascribed to our own inventions
have been the courteous revelations of spirits ;
for those noble essences in heaven bear a
friendly regard unto their fellow-nature on
earth ; and therefore believe that those many
prodigies and ominous prognostics which fore-
run the ruins of states, princes, and private
persons are the charitable premonitions of good
angels, which more careless inquiries term but
the effects of chance and nature.

ON MAN

These are certainly the magisterial and
masterpieces of the Creator, the flower, or (as

we may say) the best part of nothing, actually
existing, what we are but in hopes, and pro-
bability ; we are only that amphibious piece
between a corporeal and spiritual essence, that
middle form that links those two together, and
makes good the method of God and nature,
that jumps not from extremes, but unites the
incompatible distances by some middle and
participating natures.   That we are the breath
and similitude of God, it is indisputable, and
upon record of holy Scripture ; but to call
ourselves a microcosm, or little world, I
thought it only a pleasant trope of rhetoric,
till my near judgment and second thoughts
told me there was a real truth therein : for
first we are a rude mass, and in the rank of
creatures, which only are, and have a dull kind
of being not yet privileged with life, or preferred to sense or reason ; next we live the
life of plants, the life of animals, the life of
men, and at last the life of spirits, running
in one mysterious nature those five kinds
of existences, which comprehend the creatures
not only of the world but of the universe ;
thus is man that great and true amphibium,
whose nature is disposed to live not only like
other creatures in divers elements, but in
divided and distinguished worlds : for though

there be but one to sense, there are two to reason ; the one visible, the other invisible, whereof Moses seems to have left description, and of the other so obscurely, that some parts thereof are yet in controversy. And truly for the first chapters of Genesis, I must confess a great deal of obscurity ; though divines have to the power of human reason endeavoured to make all go in a literal meaning, yet those allegorical interpretations are also probable, and perhaps the mystical method of Moses, bred up in the hieroglyphical schools of the Egyptians.

The whole creation is a mystery, and particularly that of man. At the blast of His mouth were the rest of the creatures made, and at His bare word they started out of nothing : but in the frame of man (as the text describes it) he played the sensible operator, and seemed not so much to create, as make him. When he had separated the materials of other creatures, there consequently resulted a form and soul ; but having raised the walls of man, he was driven to a second and harder creation of a substance like himself, an incorruptible and immortal soul. . . . In our study of anatomy there is a mass of mysterious philosophy, and such as reduced the very

heathens to divinity; yet amongst all those
rare discoveries, and curious pieces I find in
the fabric of man, I do not so much content
myself, as in that I find not—that is, no organ
or instrument for the rational soul: for in the
brain, which we term the seat of reason, there
is not anything of moment more than I can
discover in the cranium of a beast: and this
is a sensible and no inconsiderable argument
of the inorganity of the soul, at least in that
sense we usually so conceive it. Thus we are
men, and we know not how; there is something in us that can be without us, and will be
after us, though it is strange that it hath no
history what it was before us, nor cannot tell
how it entered in us.

ON NATURE

Thus there are two books from whence I
collect my divinity—besides that written one of
God, another of His servant nature; that universal and public manuscript, that lies expanded
unto the eyes of all—those that never saw Him
in the one, have discovered Him in the other.
This was the scripture and theology of the
heathens; the natural motion of the sun made
them more admire Him, than its supernatural

station did the children of Israel ; the ordinary effects of nature wrought more admiration in them than in the other all His miracles : surely the heathens knew better how to join and read these mystical letters, than we Christians, who cast a more careless eye on these common hieroglyphics, and disdain to suck divinity from the flowers of nature. Nor do I so forget God as to adore the name of nature; which I define not with the schools, to be the principle of motion and rest, but that straight and regular line, that settled and constant course the wisdom of God hath ordained the actions of His creatures, according to their several kinds. To make a revolution every day, is the nature of the sun, because of that necessary course which God hath ordained it, from which it cannot swerve, by a faculty from that voice which first did give it motion. Now this course of nature God seldom alters or perverts, but like an excellent artist hath so contrived His work, that with the selfsame instrument, without a new creation, He may effect His obscurest designs. Thus He sweeteneth the water with a wood, preserveth the creatures in the ark, which the blast of His mouth might have as easily created ; for God is like a skilful geometrician, who when more easily, and with one stroke of his compass, he might describe or divide a right line, had yet rather to do this in a circle or longer way, according to the constituted and fore-laid principles of his art : yet this rule of His He doth sometimes pervert, to acquaint the world with His prerogative, lest the arrogancy of our reason should question His power, and conclude He could not. And thus I call the effects of nature the works of God, whose hand and instrument she only is ; and therefore to ascribe His actions unto her, is to devolve the honour of the principal agent upon the instrument ; which, if with reason we may do, then let our hammers rise up and boast they have built our houses, and our pens receive the honour of our writing. . . . Now nature is not at variance with art, nor art with nature : they being both servants of His providence. Art is the perfection of nature : were the world now as it was the sixth day, there were yet a chaos. Nature hath made one world, and art another. In brief, all things are artificial ; for nature is the art of God.

ON PHILOSOPHY

Beware of philosophy, is a precept not to be received in too large a sense ; for in this mass

of nature there is a set of things that carry in
their front, though not in capital letters, yet in
stenography, and short characters, something
of divinity, which to wiser reasons serve as
luminaries in the abyss of knowledge, and to
judicious beliefs, as scales and rundles to mount
the pinnacles and highest pieces of divinity.
The severe schools shall never laugh me out of
the philosophy of Hermes, that this visible
world is but a picture of the invisible, wherein,
as in a portrait, things are not truly, but in
equivocal shapes, and as they counterfeit some
real substance in that invisible fabric.

ON FINAL CAUSE

There is but one first cause, and four second
causes of all things ; some are without efficient,
as God ; others without matter, as angels ;
some without form, as the first matter : but
every essence, created or uncreated, hath its
final cause, and some positive end both of its
essence and operation ; this is the cause I grope
after in the works of nature ; on this hangs the
providence of God. To raise so beauteous a
structure, as the world and the creatures thereof, was but His art ; but their sundry and
divided operations, with their predestinated

ends, are from the treasure of His wisdom. In
the causes, nature, and affections of the eclipses
of the sun and moon, there is most excellent
speculation ; but to profound farther, and to
contemplate a reason why His providence hath
so disposed and ordered their motions in that
vast circle, as to conjoin and obscure each
other, is a sweeter piece of reason, and a
diviner point of philosophy ; therefore sometimes, and in some things, there appears to me as
much divinity in Galen's books *De Usu Partium*,
as in Suarez's Metaphysics : had Aristotle been
as curious in the inquiry of this cause as he
was of the other, he had not left behind him
an imperfect piece of philosophy, but an absolute tract of divinity.

ON DEATH

This is that dismal conquest we all deplore,
that makes us so often cry, O Adam, *quid
fecisti ?* I thank God I have not those straight
ligaments or narrow obligations to the world
as to dote on life, or be convulsed and tremble
at the name of death. Not that I am insensible
of the dread and horror thereof, or by raking
into the bowels of the deceased, continual sight
of anatomies, skeletons, or cadaverous relics,

like vespilloes, or grave-makers, I am become stupid, or have forgot the apprehension of mortality ; but that marshalling all the horrors, and contemplating the extremities thereof, I find not anything therein able to daunt the courage of a man, much less a well-resolved Christian. And therefore am not angry at the error of our first parents, or unwilling to bear a part of this common fate, and like the best of them to die, that is, to cease to breathe, to take a farewell of the elements, to be a kind of nothing for a moment, to be within one instant of a spirit. When I take a full view and circle of myself, without this reasonable moderator and equal piece of justice, death, I do conceive myself the miserablest person extant. Were there not another life that I hope for, all the vanities of this world should not entreat a moment's breath for me ; could the devil work my belief to imagine I could never die, I would not outlive that very thought; I have so abject a conceit of this common way of existence, this retaining to the sun and elements, I cannot think this is to be a man, or to live according to the dignity of humanity. In expectation of a better, I can with patience embrace this life, yet in my best meditations do often desire death. I honour any man that contemns it,

nor can I highly love any that is afraid of it :
this makes me naturally love a soldier, and
honour those tattered and contemptible regi-
ments that will die at the command of a
sergeant. For a pagan there may be some
motives to be in love with life ; but for a
Christian to be amazed at death, I see not how
he can escape this dilemma, that he is too
sensible of this life or hopeless of the life to
come.

I am naturally bashful, nor hath conversation,
age, or travel, been able to effront or enharden
me ; yet I have one part of modesty which I
have seldom discovered in another, that is,
(to speak truly,) I am not so much afraid of
death, as ashamed thereof. It is the very
disgrace and ignominy of our natures, that in
a moment can so disfigure us, that our nearest
friends, wife and children stand afraid and start
at us. The birds and beasts of the field, that
before in a natural fear obeyed us, forgetting
all allegiance, begin to prey upon us. This
very conceit hath in a tempest disposed and
left me willing to be swallowed up in the abyss
of waters ; wherein I had perished unseen,
unpitied, without wondering eyes, tears of
pity, lectures of mortality, and none had said,
Quantum mutatus ab illo ! Not that I am

ashamed of the anatomy of my parts, or can
accuse nature for playing the bungler in any
part of me, or my own vicious life for contract-
ing any shameful disease upon me, whereby I
might not call myself as wholesome a morsel
for the worms as any.

ON HEAVEN

Now, the necessary mansions of our restored
selves are those two contrary and incompatible
places we call heaven and hell; to define them,
or strictly to determine what and where these
are, surpasseth my divinity. That elegant
apostle which seemed to have a glimpse of
heaven hath left but a negative description
thereof: 'which neither eye hath seen, nor ear
hath heard, nor can enter into the heart of
man': he was translated out of himself to
behold it; but being returned into himself
could not express it. St. John's description
by emeralds, chrysolites, and precious stones
is too weak to express the material heaven we
behold. Briefly, therefore, where the soul
hath the full measure and complement of
happiness, where the boundless appetite of
that spirit remains completely satisfied that
it can neither desire addition nor alteration,

that I think is truly heaven : and this can only
be in the enjoyment of that essence whose
infinite goodness is able to terminate the
desires of itself, and the insatiable wishes of
ours ; wherever God will thus manifest Himself, there is heaven, though within the circle
of this sensible world.   Thus the soul of man
may be in heaven anywhere, even within the
limits of his own proper body ; and when it
ceaseth to live in the body it may remain in
its own soul, that is, its Creator.   And thus
we may say that St. Paul, whether in the body,
or out of the body, was yet in heaven. . . .
Moses, that was bred up in all the learning of
the Egyptians, committed a gross absurdity in
philosophy when with these eyes of flesh he
desired to see God, and petitioned his Maker,
that is truth itself, to a contradiction.

ON HELL

Men commonly set forth the torments of
hell by fire, and the extremity of corporeal
afflictions, and describe hell in the same method
that Mahomet doth heaven.   This indeed
makes a noise, and drums in popular ears ;
but if this be the terrible piece thereof, it is
not worthy to stand in diameter with heaven,

whose happiness consists in that part that is best able to comprehend it, that immortal essence, that translated divinity and colony of God, the soul. Surely, though we place hell under earth, the devil's walk and purlieu is about it : men speak too popularly who place it in those flaming mountains, which to grosser apprehensions represent hell. The heart of man is the place the devils dwell in. I feel sometimes a hell within myself; Lucifer keeps his court in my breast ; Legion is revived in me. There are as many hells as Anaxagoras conceited worlds. There was more than one hell in Magdalene, when there were seven devils ; for every devil is a hell unto himself. He holds enough of torture in his own *ubi*, and needs not the misery of circumference to afflict him. And thus, a distracted conscience here, is a shadow or introduction unto hell hereafter. Who can but pity the merciful intention of those hands that do destroy themselves? The devil, were it in his power, would do the like ; which being impossible, his miseries are endless, and he suffers most in that attribute wherein he is impassible—his immortality.

I thank God that (with joy I mention it) I was never afraid of hell, nor never grew pale at the description of that place. I have so

fixed my contemplations on heaven, that I
have almost forgot the idea of hell, and am
afraid rather to lose the joys of the one, than
endure the misery of the other—to be deprived
of them is a perfect hell, and needs, methinks,
no addition to complete our afflictions. That
terrible term hath never detained me from sin,
nor do I owe any good action to the name
thereof. I fear God, yet am not afraid of
Him ; His mercies make me ashamed of my
sins, before His judgments afraid thereof.
These are the forced and secondary methods
of His wisdom, which He useth but as the last
remedy, and upon provocation ; a course rather
to deter the wicked, than incite the virtuous
to His worship. I can hardly think there was
ever any scared into heaven : they go the
fairest way to heaven that would serve God
without a hell. Other mercenaries that crouch
unto Him, in fear of hell, though they term
themselves the servants, are indeed but the
slaves of the Almighty.

ON PRAYER

I cannot contentedly frame a prayer for
myself in particular, without a catalogue for
my friends ; nor request a happiness wherein

my sociable disposition doth not desire the fellowship of my neighbour. I never heard the toll of a passing-bell, though in my mirth, without my prayers and best wishes for the departing spirit. I cannot go to cure the body of my patient, but I forget my profession, and call unto God for his soul. I cannot see one say his prayers, but instead of imitating him, I fall into a supplication for him, who, perhaps, is no more to me than a common nature; and if God hath vouchsafed an ear to my supplications, there are surely many happy that never saw me, and enjoy the blessing of my unknown devotions. To pray for enemies, that is, for their salvation, is no harsh precept, but the practice of our daily and ordinary devotions.

ON CHARITY

The vulgarity of those judgments that wrap the Church of God in Strabo's cloak, and restrain it unto Europe, seem to me as bad geographers as Alexander, who thought he had conquered all the world, when he had not subdued the half of any part thereof. For we cannot deny the Church of God both in Asia and Africa, if we do not forget the peregrinations of the apostles, the deaths of the martyrs, the sessions of many, and, even in our reformed judgment, lawful councils, held in those parts in the minority and nonage of ours. Nor must a few differences, more remarkable in the eyes of man than perhaps in the judgment of God, excommunicate from heaven one another, much less those Christians who are in a manner all martyrs, maintaining their faith in the noble way of persecution, and serving God in the fire, whereas we honour Him in the sunshine. It is true we all hold there is a number of elect, and many to be saved ; yet take our opinions together, and from the confusion thereof there will be no such thing as salvation, nor shall any one be saved. For first, the Church of Rome condemneth us, we likewise them ; the sub-reformists and sectaries sentence the doctrine of our Church as damnable ; the atomist, or familist, reprobates all these ; and all these them again. Thus, whilst the mercies of God do promise us heaven, our conceits and opinions exclude us from that place. There must be therefore more than one St. Peter. Particular churches and sects usurp the gates of heaven, and turn the key against each other : and thus we go to heaven against each other's wills, conceits, and opinions, and, with as much uncharity as ignorance, do err, I fear, in points not only of our own, but one another's salvation.

I believe many are saved, who to man seem reprobated; and many are reprobated who in the opinion and sentence of man stand elected. There will appear at the last day strange and unexpected examples, both of His justice and His mercy; and therefore to define either is folly in man, and insolency even in the devils. Those acute and subtle spirits, in all their sagacity, can hardly divine who shall be saved; which if they could prognosticate, their labour were at an end; nor need they compass the earth, seeking whom they may devour. Those who, upon a rigid application of the law, sentence Solomon unto damnation, condemn not only him but themselves, and the whole world; for by the letter, and written word of God, we are, without exception, in the state of death; but there is a prerogative of God, and an arbitrary pleasure above the letter of His own law, by which alone we can pretend unto salvation, and through which Solomon might be as easily saved as those who condemn him.

The number of those who pretend unto salvation, and those infinite swarms who think to pass through the eye of this needle, have much amazed me. That name and compellation of 'little flock' doth not comfort but deject my devotion, especially when I reflect upon mine own unworthiness, wherein, according to my humble apprehensions, I am below them all. I believe there shall never be an anarchy in heaven ; but as there are hierarchies amongst the angels, so shall there be degrees of priority amongst the saints. Yet it is, I protest, beyond my ambition to aspire unto the first ranks ; my desires only are, and I shall be happy therein, to be but the last man, and bring up the rear in heaven.

ON THE REFORMATION

As there were many reformers, so likewise many reformations ; every country proceeding in a particular way and method, according as their national interest, together with their constitution and clime inclined them ; some angrily, and with extremity ; others calmly, and with mediocrity, not rending, but easily dividing the community, and leaving an honest possibility of a reconciliation ; which, though peaceable spirits do desire, and may conceive that revolution of time and the mercies of God may effect, yet that judgment that shall consider the present antipathies between the two extremes, their contrarieties in condition, affection, and opinion, may with the same hopes expect a union in the poles of heaven.

It is the promise of Christ to make us all one flock ; but how, and when this union shall be, is as obscure to me as the last day.

ON A DYING PATIENT OF HIS

Upon my first visit I was bold to tell them who had not let fall all hopes of his recovery, that in my sad opinion he was not like to behold a grasshopper, much less to pluck another fig ; and in no long time after seemed to discover that odd mortal symptom in him not mentioned by Hippocrates, that is, to lose his own face, and look like some of his near relations ; for he maintained not his proper countenance, but looked like his uncle, the lines of whose face lay deep and invisible in his healthful visage before : for as from our beginning we run through variety of looks, before we come to consistent and settled faces ; so before our end, by sick and languishing alterations, we put on new visages : and in our retreat to earth, may fall upon such looks which from community of seminal originals were before latent in us.

Not to fear death, nor desire it, was short of his resolution : to be dissolved, and be with Christ, was his dying ditty. He conceived his thread long, in no long course of years, and when he had scarce outlived the second life of Lazarus ; esteeming it enough to approach the years of his Saviour, who so ordered His own human state as not to be old upon earth.

Though age had set no seal upon his face, yet a dim eye might clearly discover fifty in his actions ; and therefore, since wisdom is the grey hair, and an unspotted life old age ; although his years came short, he might have been said to have held up with longer livers, and to have been Solomon's old man. And surely if we deduct all those days of our life which we might wish unlived, and which abate the comfort of those we now live ; if we reckon up only those days which God hath accepted of our lives, a life of good years will hardly be a span long : the son in this sense may outlive the father, and none be climacterically old. He that early arriveth unto the parts and prudence of age, is happily old without the uncomfortable attendants of it ; and 'tis superfluous to live unto grey hairs, when in a precocious temper we anticipate the virtues of them. In brief, he cannot be accounted young who out-

liveth the old man.   He that hath early arrived
unto the measure of a perfect stature in Christ,
hath already fulfilled the prime and longest
intention of his being : and one day lived after
the perfect rule of piety, is to be preferred
before sinning immortality.

ON A HEAVENLY MIND

Lastly; if length of days be thy portion,
make it not thy expectation.   Reckon not
upon long life : think every day the last, and
live always beyond thy account.   He that so
often surviveth his expectation lives many lives,
and will scarce complain of the shortness of
his days.   Time past is gone like a shadow ;
make time to come present.   Approximate thy
latter times by present apprehensions of them :
be like a neighbour unto the grave, and think
there is but little to come.   And since there
is something of us that will still live on,
join both lives together, and live in one but
for the other.   He who thus ordereth the
purposes of this life, will never be far from the
next ; and is in some manner already in it, by
a happy conformity and close apprehension of
it.   And if, as we have elsewhere declared,

any have been so happy, as personally to understand Christian annihilation, ecstasy, exolution,
transformation, the kiss of the spouse, and
ingression into the divine shadow, according to
mystical theology, they have already had an
handsome anticipation of heaven ; the world is
in a manner over, and the earth in ashes unto
them.

ON THE RELIGIO MEDICI

This I confess, about seven years past, with
some others of affinity thereto, for my private
exercise and satisfaction I had at leisurable hours
composed ; which being communicated unto
one, it became common unto many, and was
by transcription successively corrupted, until it
arrived in a most depraved copy at the press.
He that shall peruse that work, and shall take
notice of sundry particulars and personal expressions therein, will easily discern the intention was not public : and being a private
exercise directed to myself, what is delivered
therein, was rather a memorial unto me, than
an example or rule unto any other : and therefore if there be any singularity therein corre-
spondent unto the private conceptions of any
man, it doth not advantage them : or if dis-

sentaneous thereunto, it no way overthrows them.   It was penned in such a place, and with such disadvantage, that (I protest) from the first setting of pen unto paper, I had not the assistance of any good book, whereby to promote my invention, or relieve my memory, and therefore there might be many real lapses therein, which others might take notice of, and more than I suspected myself.   It was set down many years past, and was the sense of my conception at that time, not an immutable law unto my advancing judgment at all times; and therefore there might be many things therein plausible unto my past apprehension, which are not agreeable unto my present self.   There are many things delivered rhetorically, many expressions therein merely tropical, and as they best illustrate my intention, and therefore also there are many things to be taken in a soft and flexible sense and not to be called unto the rigid test of reason.   Lastly, all that is contained therein, is in submission unto maturer discernments ; and as I have declared, shall no further father them than the best and learned judgments shall authorise them ; under favour of which considerations I have made its secrecy public, and committed the truth thereof to every ingenuous reader.

LAST LINES OF THE RELIGIO MEDICI

Bless me in this life with but peace of my conscience, command of my affections, the love of Thyself and my dearest friends, and I shall be happy enough to pity Cæsar. These are, O Lord, the humble desires of my most reasonable ambition, and all I dare call happiness on earth ; wherein I set no rule or limit to Thy hand of Providence ; dispose of me according to the wisdom of Thy pleasure. Thy will be done, though in my own undoing.